GW01471573

PHYSICAL PROCESSES

CONTENTS

About this book

Welcome to *Resource Bank: Physical Processes*. Our aim in writing this book has been to draw on our experience as teachers to provide you with practical lessons. These lessons will help you to explore electricity, forces and motion, and light and sound with your class.

Where appropriate, we have added hints and tips to help you avoid some of the mistakes that we made when we first tried practical science activities with young children. We hope that you will adapt the activities in the light of your own professional experience and personal knowledge of the children with whom you work.

As we wrote this book, we were aware that physical processes is an area of science in which many teachers feel they do not have a sufficient depth of subject knowledge. This means that ideas for lessons can be more difficult to generate, and consequently more time-consuming to prepare. We have tried to take this into account when writing the activities. The science in all of these lessons is based on real-life contexts that are likely to relate to the children's experience. The full-colour A1 'birthday party' poster provided in the centre of this book acts as a stimulus for many lessons, and is a reminder that science is about observing the real world and understanding how it works.

We think science is great fun – and as children are naturally inquisitive, they will be keen to experiment with and extend the ideas you offer them. We hope that the activities in this book will provide you with many hours of enjoyable science in your classroom, as they have in ours.

INTRODUCTION

Teaching about physical processes

When we teach the 'Physical processes' strand of science to young children, we should remember that the concepts we are helping the children to develop are seldom part of a child's daily conversation. Nevertheless, all children will have experiences on which they can build their understanding. Forces, electricity, light and sound are all around us. We experience and use them every day, but we seldom stop to reflect on them and the ways in which they influence our daily lives.

In helping children to understand how the real world works, we need to provide appropriate vocabulary which they can use to ask questions and communicate their understanding. Young children learn in a variety of ways, but the role of play and practical, hands-on experience cannot be overstated. Through play, and discussion about their play, children will learn kinaesthetically, collect visual images that will aid memory and have their learning reinforced through spoken language.

Some common misconceptions

As teachers, we need to be aware of children's misconceptions in science. For example, in the activity 'Hall of mirrors' (page 25), many children will believe the mirror to be a light source. Research informs us that children will not easily cast off such misconceptions. In order to modify their models of the world, they need to be convinced that their models are inadequate – that is, that they do not satisfactorily explain the phenomena being observed. Research also indicates that the teacher simply telling them they are wrong does not rectify their misconceptions!

Children (and adults) need to build their understanding on a spiral of learning experiences that gradually adds pieces to the mental jigsaw until the wider picture takes shape. We have found, for example, that children sometimes begin to modify their misconception about mirrors when they are looking at their own reflection. In the activity 'Hall of mirrors', try asking the children to look at themselves in the mirror and to talk about their own reflection: *Where is the light that helps you see yourself in the mirror coming from?*

When helping children to modify their misconceptions, always try to relate the learning to something that the child already knows. In the example above, the children will have experience of looking at themselves in mirrors and will probably be aware that they are looking at a reflection of themselves. From this starting point, you may be able to build an understanding that the mirror reflects a torch when it is switched on.

Another common misconception involves the children's understanding of shadows. Some children will say that they are solely responsible for making their own shadows. They deny the involvement of the Sun (or other light source) in the process. This is a symptom of the egocentricity and lack of experience of children in this age group. Try taking the children inside and asking them to 'make' their own shadow. When they find they cannot make the shadow without a light source, you may be able to help them develop a less egocentric view.

In summary, we must be very careful not to impose our own ideas on children: we must help them to gain experience for themselves, which is the only way they can develop their understanding. As teachers, we are responsible for selecting the right experiences to consolidate their learning.

Using other adults in class

The ideas in this book have been taught to children throughout KS1/P1–3. After due consideration and adaptation, they should meet your needs for children across a wide range of abilities. Our experience has shown that some of the activities require additional adults in the classroom; this further support will enhance the children's learning experience.

Science investigation

Finally, we must remember that we are responsible for maintaining the important balance between the development of scientific understanding and that of investigation skills. Science helps children to develop skills that are useful across the curriculum, and it is important that we should not become solely focused on knowledge of concepts or content to the detriment of skills development and the spirit of wonder and enquiry.

Preparing to use the poster

After you have completed the activity opposite, we suggest that you display the poster in the classroom to give the children time to absorb some of its details. As you are unlikely to cover all the 'Physical processes' strand of science in one block of time, we suggest that the poster is used recurrently as a flexible resource.

INTRODUCTION

LET'S LOOK AT THE POSTER

W

GROUP SIZE AND ORGANIZATION
Whole-class discussion.
DURATION
20 minutes.
LEARNING OBJECTIVES
To assess the children's prior knowledge. To introduce them to the poster accompanying this book.

YOU WILL NEED
The 'Birthday party' poster; a notepad and pen. (If you wish to structure your observations, you could create headings based on the skills outlined in 'Assessment'.)

SAFETY
The children are encouraged to assess risks as part of this lesson.

WHAT TO DO
Fold the poster in half, so that the right-hand side is hidden from view. Ask the children to look at the poster and to try to find five things that move. After about ten seconds of looking time, take some quick responses. Now ask them to look for more things that move: *I'll give you five more seconds to find something that no one else has mentioned.* Note the more able children who make less obvious observations or inferences. For example, does anyone suggest that the door will move, the fan moves when it is switched on, or the tree might be blown by the wind?

Now ask the children to think about safety. If they were in a garden like the one in the poster, where might it be dangerous to stand? Help them to consider the safe use of the climbing frame and the proximity of

other toys to the swings. Can they see any items in the picture that they know they must not touch? Make a note of those children who are unable to make judgements about safety, as they may need additional supervision in subsequent lessons. Asking the children whose job it is to keep them safe can sometimes stimulate an interesting discussion.

Now ask the children whether they can guess what is on the other half of the poster, then open it up so that the whole poster is showing. Focus discussion on what the children in the picture are doing. Help the children to create a long list of verbs:

The children are   singing
laughing
playing
bouncing

Encourage the children to think about themselves and what they are doing as they sit in front of you. Is there anyone who suggests *breathing, swallowing, living?* Ask:
◆ *Which of the actions uses up the most energy?*
◆ *Does anyone know where you get your energy from?*
◆ *How do you feel when you've used up lots of energy, perhaps by bouncing on a bouncy castle?*

Give the children a few seconds to take one last look at the poster. Ask them to make up a good question that they could ask you when the poster has been taken away. Warn them that you might also ask them a question when it is taken away, so they should look really carefully. Then take the poster down.

Asking questions is a high-level skill, and can be very revealing. If this is something that the children do not practise a lot, you may need to be ready with a prompt or an initial question such as:
◆ *Was the boy playing swingball wearing a hat?*
◆ *How old was the birthday boy?*
◆ *How many balloons were tied to the bike?*

ASSESSMENT
The discussion topics should give you an opportunity to make an initial assessment of some individuals' ability in science. If a helper or a member of staff observes your lesson, it may be helpful to share your assessments with them. The questions have focused on the skills of observation, raising questions and personal safety. They have been drawn from the scientific context 'Forces and motion'. The remainder of this book provides you with opportunities to help your pupils develop their skills and conceptual knowledge in this and other areas of science.

IDEAS FOR DISPLAY
Use the verb list (see above) to create an illustrated poem for classroom display.

ELECTRICITY

USING ELECTRICITY

GROUP SIZE AND ORGANIZATION
Whole class.
DURATION
40 minutes.
LEARNING OBJECTIVE
To recognize appliances that use electricity.

YOU WILL NEED
The 'Birthday party' poster and 'Living Room', 'Kitchen' and 'Fairground' mini-posters; pictures of electrical appliances and other household goods cut from magazines and catalogues; copies of an A3-sized version of the house diagram below; adhesive.

SAFETY
This activity provides an important opportunity to talk to the children about how dangerous electricity can be. The clear message must be that no children at Key Stage 1 should be touching any mains sockets at any time. Emphasize the dangers of plugs, trailing wires and wet hands.

WHAT TO DO
Look at the 'Birthday party' poster together. Identify things in the picture that use electricity (tools,

lawnmower and light bulb in the shed; fan, washing machine, fridge-freezer and cooker in the kitchen; lights on the wall of the house; camcorder). Ask the children why there is a gate on the shed; emphasize its safety value. Go on to identify things in the 'Kitchen' and 'Living-room' mini-posters that use electricity. Look at the 'Fairground' mini-poster together; help the children to appreciate that electricity will bring the fairground to life with lights, sounds and movements!

Encourage the children to think about what things in the classroom use electricity. Give them the collection of pictures and copies of the house diagram, and ask them to place only the electrical items into the appropriate rooms in the house. Say that some of the items may not be electrical. When they are sure where to place the items, they can stick them down.

When they have completed the activity, discuss appliances that are usually found only in one room (such as a fridge) and others that are not room-specific (such as a TV set).

ASSESSMENT
By looking at the children's completed houses, you can assess whether they can identify electrical appliances. They should not have stuck down the pictures of non-electrical goods.

IDEAS FOR DIFFERENTIATION
More able children could be given pages from magazines and catalogues, so they have to identify and cut out the pictures themselves.

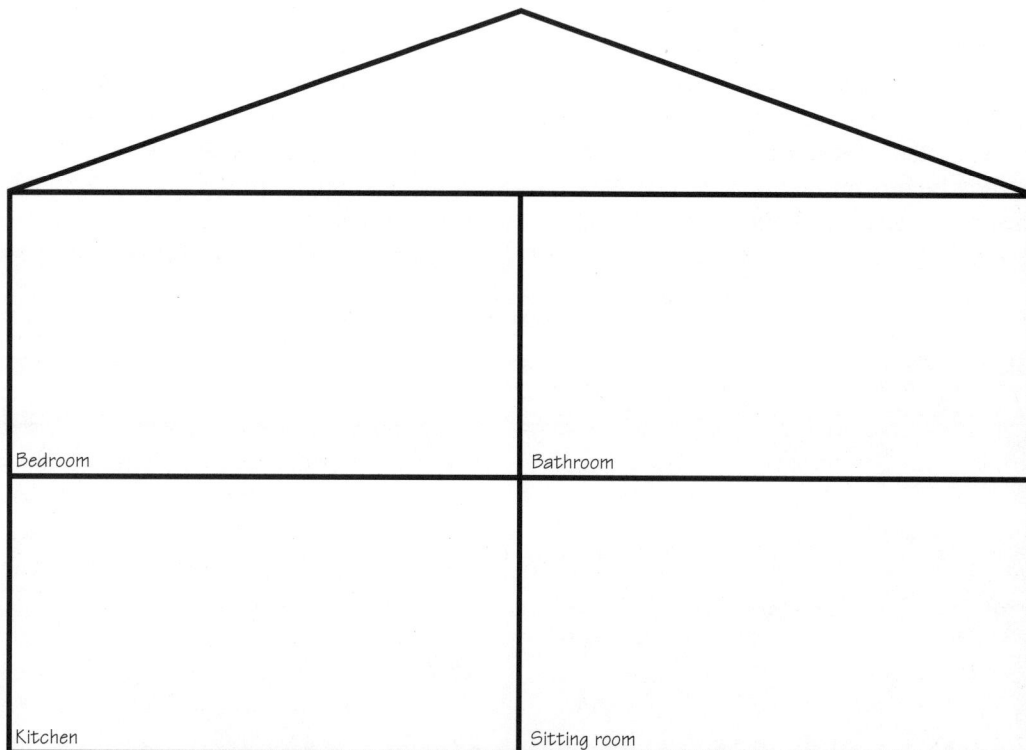

Bedroom

Bathroom

Kitchen

Sitting room

ELECTRICITY

CIRCUITS

GROUP SIZE AND ORGANIZATION
Whole class, then groups of up to ten children working in rotation.
DURATION
30 minutes for each group.
LEARNING OBJECTIVE
To know that a bulb, battery and wires can be joined to form a simple circuit and make a bulb light up.

YOU WILL NEED
The 'Birthday Party' poster; a collection including at least some of the following: thin insulated wire, thin wire from which the insulation has been removed, crocodile clips, string, shoelaces, kitchen foil, wire strippers.

You will also need one battery and one bulb in a holder for each child (or pair), plus a few spares. Use 4.5V batteries (EverReady 1289 or equivalent), which have two terminals for ease of connection; 3.5V bulbs will work effectively with these.

SAFETY
The activity 'Using electricity' (page 4) provides an opportunity to discuss the dangers of mains electricity. The warnings should be reinforced at the beginning of this lesson.

There is also some risk from the glass bulbs. A child once chewed a bulb in our lesson; and on a number of occasions bulbs have been broken and caused minor cuts. You need to consider these factors when assessing the level of risk for your class.

Please do not use rechargeable cells (batteries) for this lesson, as they can be short-circuited and generate high temperatures.

WHAT TO DO
Talk to the whole class about safety and electricity.

Gather the children around the 'Birthday Party' poster. Identify the sources of light in the picture (candles, bulb in shed, lights on wall of house). Help the children to identify which of these are powered by electricity.

Now show the children a piece of insulated electrical wire. Ask them what is inside the plastic coating. Do they know that the metal wire runs all the way through? Use the wire strippers to show the wire. Explain that electricity flows through metal wires to make bulbs light up.

Set the children in groups the challenge of lighting a bulb for themselves. Allow them 10–15 minutes to work with the collection of materials. Stay with the group and watch them progress. If someone lights their bulb quickly, ask them to share their solution with the rest of the group. If no one has made a bulb light and some children are reaching frustration point, intervene and demonstrate a circuit yourself.

As they continue to investigate, encourage the children to try all the materials that you have provided. For example, they can use strips of kitchen foil in place of wires. Ask:
◆ What is making the bulb light? (A complete circuit with wires, bulb and battery.)
◆ Which materials will allow the electricity to pass through them? (The metal ones.)
◆ Can you explain why the bulb does not light up when string is used in the circuit? (String does not conduct electricity.)

Draw the children together by taking them away from the collection of materials. Talk with them about their discoveries, and try to rectify any misconceptions. Ask them to think about the lights in the classroom: Do you know where the wires go? Finally, re-emphasize the dangers of mains electricity.

ELECTRICITY

ASSESSMENT
Record which children were good at answering questions, and which will require more teaching.

IDEAS FOR DISPLAY
The collection of materials, together with one battery and bulb, can be left out for a few days to allow further investigation. You could add a buzzer or motor to extend the children's knowledge. You may also wish to provide some simple questions (perhaps on cards) as a focus for investigation, such as:
◆ *Can you light the bulb?*
◆ *Which materials can you use to light the bulb?*
◆ *Is the bulb always as bright when you use a different material?*

IDEAS FOR DIFFERENTIATION
Note those children who would benefit from additional teaching on this topic in subsequent lessons.

EXTENSION WORK
Let the children investigate circuits including buzzers and motors.

CANDLES ON THE CAKE

GROUP SIZE AND ORGANIZATION
Whole-class introduction; groups of up to ten children, working in pairs.
DURATION
35 minutes.
LEARNING OBJECTIVE
To know that several bulbs can be lit in series, using a simple circuit.

YOU WILL NEED
The 'Birthday party' poster; the 'Fairground' mini-poster; a circuit containing a single bulb.

Each pair of children in the science group will need: one 4.5V battery (EverReady 1289 or equivalent); two 3.5V bulbs and holders; three wires with crocodile clips. You will need access to some additional wire and wire strippers, so that the children's circuits can be extended as necessary.

Each individual in the candle-making group will need: a small tube of card (about the size of a standard tube of Smarties) or a strip of card that can be rolled into a tube; materials to decorate the tubes; tissue paper.

Before the lesson, cut a strip of white card and form it into a circle with the same diameter as a paper plate. This will be the 'cake', and the plate will be the lid through which the children's candles will be pushed (you could prepare the holes in the lid). Prepare enough cakes for your class. For a class of 30 children, five cakes will work well (six candles per cake).

SAFETY
If your children have followed the previous lessons in this section of the book, they should be well aware of the risks connected with mains electricity. Nevertheless, we feel that we would never undertake a lesson including electrical apparatus without discussing safety issues. In this lesson, we leave you to judge which aspects of safety you wish to reinforce.

WHAT TO DO
Gather all the children to look at the 'Birthday party' poster. Talk to them about the lights attached to the wall of the house. Ask questions such as:
◆ *Have you seen lights in a row like this before? Where?* (Lights for Christmas or Diwali in the street or on trees.)
◆ *Do you think we could make a series of lights work in a row like this, using our batteries and bulbs?*
Look together at the black and white 'Fairground' mini-poster. How many rows or circles of electric lights can the children see?

At this point, bring out a prepared circuit containing a single bulb and hold it so that the children can see that the bulb is lit. Remind the children that to make the bulb light in the 'Circuits' activity (see page 5), they had to create a circuit with metal wires and a battery.

Now split the children into three working groups. With a class of 30 children, it is possible to rotate the

ELECTRICITY

groups so that all the children will have completed the science activity in one afternoon. Tell the children what each group will be doing during the session: the first group carry out the science work; the second group make and decorate candle shapes; the third group follow your usual class self-sustaining activities (such as role-play or working with construction toys).

Give the science group their materials, telling them that they are to work in pairs and that they can only use the materials they have been given. Set the challenge: to light both bulbs using only one battery. Insist that they must not borrow any materials from any other children.

Work briefly with the second group who are making and decorating the candles. Make sure they understand that they are going to make 'pretend' candles to put on a 'pretend' birthday cake. They can use tissue paper as a decoration and to stuff the tube once the wires are in place. If there is time, ask them to identify some differences between a real candle and a bulb:

◆ *Tell me something about a candle's light that is different from the light made by this bulb.* (The candle has a flame; it can burn you directly; the bulb is made from glass; the bulb needs wires.)
◆ *How do you light a real candle?* (You need a match, lighter or other source of flame.)

Now return to the science group and give them feedback on their progress. Help each pair to solve the problem. Explain to this group that they are going to use what they have found out to make pretend candles. Now rotate the groups, so that the science group can move to the candle-making area.

As the session progresses, stop the children to reinforce the learning that is taking place. As each pair of children finish their pair of candles, fit these into the birthday cake lid (the paper plate).

ASSESSMENT
Identify those children who can or cannot wire the bulbs correctly in series. Can they explain where the electricity is stored? (In the battery.) Can they show you a complete circuit?

IDEAS FOR DISPLAY
◆ When the cakes have been completed, put them on display so that the wires from the candles stick out under the edge of each cake. Leave a battery with the display, and encourage the children to guess which wires will light which candles.
◆ The cakes could be placed in front of a board displaying the 'Birthday party' poster. Finally, you could use a set of electric lights to add a colourful border.

IDEAS FOR DIFFERENTIATION
◆ Children who find the construction of the circuit difficult may require more adult support. The modelling aspects of the lesson can be simplified by providing ready-prepared tubes for children to decorate.
◆ More able children can be encouraged to work in groups of four to explore the number of bulbs that they can put in a series powered by a single battery.

EXTENSION WORK
Ask the children to think about ways in which they could switch their 'candles' on and off. Provide them with some commercially produced switches so that they can experiment with these in their circuits.

FORCES AND MOTION

SKITTLES, BEANBAGS, BALLS AND HOOPS

GROUP SIZE AND ORGANIZATION
Whole class in playground and classroom.
DURATION
Up to 1 hour.
LEARNING OBJECTIVE
To describe the movement of familiar objects.

YOU WILL NEED
The 'Birthday party' poster; skittles; balls (for skittles); larger balls; beanbags; hoops; access to the playground; a flipchart (or four large pieces of paper); marker pens; photocopiable page 19 (see 'Ideas for differentiation'); paper and pencils.

SAFETY
This lesson carries the risks inherent in any outdoor PE lesson. The children should be reminded to behave sensibly so as not to injure themselves or others.

WHAT TO DO
Gather the children around the 'Birthday party' poster in the classroom, with the flipchart nearby. Ask them to look at the skittles game on the poster:
◆ *What is happening to the skittles as the ball hits them?*
◆ *How are the skittles moving?*
Extend the children's use of language as appropriate (for example: *falling over, knocking into, flying through the air, moving quickly*). Now consider the movement of the ball. Ask the children to imagine the ball travelling towards the skittles. *How does it move across the ground?* As the children offer suggestions (such as 'bounce' and 'roll'), make notes of good words on the flipchart. Tell the children that the lesson will help them to make a useful collection of 'movement words' (or, if you prefer, 'travelling words').

Now take the flipchart outside with the children. Let some children demonstrate the movement of the skittles by rolling the ball at a group of skittles. Were the children's word predictions correct? Can they think of new words to describe the movement?

Divide the playground into four sectors, each containing a different set of apparatus: skittles and balls; larger balls; hoops; beanbags. Split the children into four groups, reminding them that they should try to think of good words to describe the movement of the items in their sector of the playground. As the words for the skittles have already been collected, you should concentrate on the remaining three sectors (the group working with the skittles are reinforcing their learning). Use a separate sheet on the flipchart for each sector, and rotate the groups around the playground to build up a good range of words.

When the children have experienced all the activities, draw the class together back in the classroom in front of the 'Birthday party' poster. Ask the children to identify some of the things in the picture that would be moving in real life (such as the balloons, the see-saw or the clouds). Now encourage the children to experiment with the collection of words. Would it be right to describe the balloon's movement as 'spinning'? They should explore the possibilities, writing unlikely sentences:
◆ *The balloon was spinning through the air.*
◆ *The clouds bounced along in the sky.*
◆ *The see-saw was rolling up and down.*
Finally, ask the children to make up some good, realistic descriptive sentences using the 'movement words'.

ASSESSMENT
The writing exercise will provide assessment opportunities. As you circulate around the class, check who can describe the movement of a range of objects that you have not covered with the class:
◆ *How do trees move in the wind?*

RESOURCE BANK

FORCES AND MOTION

◆ *How would you describe the way a door handle moves?*

◆ *How do horses move – can you think of different words?*

IDEAS FOR DISPLAY

Use the 'movement words' list to create a display about one form of movement (for example, 'Things that roll' or 'Things that bounce'). This can be changed week by week as the children create pictures and pieces of descriptive writing based on the words collected during the lesson.

IDEAS FOR DIFFERENTIATION

Support less confident children with the sentence writing activity by preparing some sentence openings. Photocopiable page 19 may be useful for this purpose. More able children could be challenged to collect their own set of movement words, perhaps as a homework activity.

EXTENSION WORK

Ask the children to imagine that they are going on a journey. They have to describe all the things they can see moving as they travel along. These descriptions can then be incorporated into a song similar to 'The Wheels on the Bus' (for example: 'The people in the park go shuffle, shuffle, shuffle / The birds in the air go flap, flap, flap / The ball in the field goes bounce, bounce, bounce...'), or into a narrative.

MOVING AIR

GROUP SIZE AND ORGANIZATION
Groups of 8 or 12.
DURATION
40 minutes.
LEARNING OBJECTIVE
To know that sucking and blowing exert forces.

YOU WILL NEED

The 'Birthday party' poster; a box of large drinking straws; a glass of water (or another cold drink of your choice); photocopiable page 20; some tables prepared for table football or hockey (game 1); some equal-sized pots and a collection of small balls of screwed-up paper in at least three distinct sizes, with the smallest just bigger than the end of a straw for game 2; an appropriate range of dried pulses for the extension activity.

SAFETY

There is a risk that children could inhale items if this activity is not appropriately prepared and supervised. You should carry out a risk assessment to decide whether additional adult support is needed. The children should be warned of the dangers of placing small objects in ears or noses. You may need to modify the activity to suit your own particular teaching situation.

WHAT TO DO

Gather the children around the 'Birthday party' poster. Focus their attention on the child in the picture who is drinking through a straw. Ask them to explain how they think a straw works:

◆ *What do you have to do to make the drink travel up the straw?*

Ask the children to pretend they are sucking through a straw and to pull air into their mouths. Then ask them to push the air out again. Demonstrate the effect of pushing air down the straw by blowing bubbles in your drink. Point out the bubbles of air travelling through the water, and explain that you have blown the air into the straw.

Now show the children that when air is blown out of or sucked up a straw, a ball of crushed paper can be blown away from or drawn towards the end of the straw. Allow the children a few minutes of free play with this activity, then call them back together. Ask them to describe what they have been doing, using the terms 'blowing' and 'sucking'.

FORCES AND MOTION

Split the children into two groups. Explain that one group will play a game using a blowing force and the other group will play a game using a sucking force; then they will swap.

Game 1: blowing force
The children can play table football or hockey with straws and paper balls. Establish how they can score in the game, then set pairs to play against each other.

Game 2: sucking force
This game is a party favourite. Give each child an equal-sized pile of screwed-up paper balls. On the command *Go!* the children race to transfer the paper balls into their own plastic pot. They are only allowed to use the sucking power of the straw: no touching of the paper balls with hands is allowed.

Now give out copies of photocopiable page 20 and ask the children to write about game 1 using the words 'suck' and 'blow.'

To draw the activity to a close, gather the children together and ask them to discuss the games they played. Ask them to think about the different-sized paper balls in game 2. Were the larger ones harder to pick up? If so, why?

ASSESSMENT
The written activity will provide evidence of understanding. Try to identify those children who are able or unable to show that the game they have been playing relies on the forces of sucking and blowing.

IDEAS FOR DIFFERENTIATION
Provide support for children who may find it difficult to engage with the written task. This support could take the form of a list of helpful words on the board or modelled writing with the group. More able children can be set the task of timing themselves as they play game 2.

EXTENSION WORK
Use a range of different-sized dried pulses for game 2, then ask the children to explain why some things are harder to lift than others (they are heavier). Check their understanding by asking them to choose pulses for their opponents to lift.

PULL OR PUSH ALONG

GROUP SIZE AND ORGANIZATION
Whole-class introduction, then small groups playing outside.
DURATION
Around 40 minutes (including 30 minutes for practical work).
LEARNING OBJECTIVE
To understand that pushes and pulls can make a load move.

YOU WILL NEED
The 'Birthday party' poster; the 'Fairground' mini-poster; some 'ride-on' toys; a toy wheelbarrow or toddler truck; some lengths of rope (such as skipping ropes); sand; a piece of board with a rope attached; a camera (optional – see 'Ideas for display').

FORCES AND MOTION

SAFETY
The children should be taught that it is not safe to lift very heavy loads. We recommend that you carry out a risk assessment for this activity, and have an additional adult who is able to watch the class while you interact with the small group and vice versa. The supervising adult should monitor the children's activities carefully to guarantee safety.

WHAT TO DO
Gather the children to look at the 'Birthday party' poster. Focus on the area showing the push and pull toys. Talk to the children to elicit their knowledge and experience of the toys shown in the picture:
◆ *What makes these toys move?*
◆ *Which toys do you push and which do you pull?*
◆ *Are there any toys that you both push and pull?*
◆ *Where else in the picture can you see things that will be pushed or pulled?*
Talk to the children about the kind of games they like to play using push and pull toys. If possible, draw from their ideas for the next part of the lesson. Many children like to shift loads from one place to another – for example, towing a trailer or pushing a pram. Alternatively, tell them that they are going to help refill the sandpit (or some other scenario that fits with your current role-play activities) Whatever the context, the challenge is for them to move some sand in small loads from one place to another, using some of the equipment provided (see above).

As the children play, encourage them to try pulling the loads of sand as well as pushing them. Can they find different ways of pulling – for example, by towing a load behind a ride-on tractor, or by dragging a load on a board? What do the children notice? Which method of moving the sand seems easiest?

At the end of the lesson, draw the children together and ask them:
◆ *Which toys were good for helping to move the sand?*
◆ *What would be the easiest way to move a lot of sand?*

Go back to the 'Birthday party' poster and identify some other features of the picture that include (or could include) pushes and pulls, such as: the flags blowing in the wind; the swings; the skittles game; the candles on the cake (when they are blown out). Look at the 'Fairground' poster: how many of the rides and other fairground attractions involve people being pushed or pulled? How many involve people pushing or pulling something?

ASSESSMENT
Make sure that the children understand the difference between pushes and pulls. How many pushes and pulls can they identify correctly in the 'Birthday party' picture (including future ones such as blowing out the candles, and potential ones such as playing on the see-saw)?

IDEAS FOR DISPLAY
Photograph the children while they carry out the activity. Display the photographs with captions to reinforce the vocabulary of 'push' and 'pull'.

IDEAS FOR DIFFERENTIATION
More able children can be challenged to try to explain the inertia they experience when moving the board loaded with sand. (It feels as though the board is 'stuck' to the ground until it starts to move – then it becomes easier to pull along.) They can compare different methods of moving a load and rank them in order of difficulty.

Children requiring support may benefit from repeating the activity in order to consolidate the important concepts addressed by this lesson.

EXTENSION WORK
Work with the children on developing ideas for ways to make a travelling load speed up or slow down. Can they connect the amount of force used with the speed achieved?

FORCES AND MOTION

SLOWING DOWN

GROUP SIZE AND ORGANIZATION
Whole-class introduction, then group activities.
DURATION
Introduction 20–25 minutes; group work over several afternoons.
LEARNING OBJECTIVE
To understand that we can slow down the movement of some objects by using forces.

YOU WILL NEED
The 'Birthday party' poster; some 'ride-on' toys, tricycles or stabilized bicycles (at least one of these should have brakes); a collection of freewheeling toys (such as roller-skates and toy cars); a flipchart; a camera (preferably instant or digital); Post-it Notes.

SAFETY
You need to carry out a risk assessment for the 'ride-on' toys activity. Consider the possible risk of falls, collisions and trapped fingers. Does your school have a policy on the wearing of protective headgear and clothing for outdoor play? We would strongly recommend the use of an appropriately trained adult to supervise this part of the activity. Encourage the children to always wear protective headgear when riding bicycles.

WHAT TO DO
Sit the children in a large circle. Focus their attention on the section of the poster containing the bicycle:
◆ *Have any of you ridden a bike?*
◆ *Who can tell us how you slow down on a bike?*

Explain that you are going to help the children to investigate how things slow down. Ask them to watch what happens as you roll a toy across the floor. Ask individuals to describe the movement:
◆ *Does the toy travel at the same speed all the time?*
◆ *Does it slow down? Does it stop? Why?*
Listen carefully to the children's responses. It is unlikely that they will fully understand why things slow down at this stage, but their suggestions will help you to assess their level of understanding. Note those children who suggest that the surface over which the toy travels may be a significant factor, and also any explanations expressed in terms that display an understanding of the force provided by the person who pushed the toy.

Show the children a different toy and ask them: *Will this toy slow down in the same way as the first toy? Why/ why not?*

Choose some children to take turns at rolling different toys across the floor. Use the flipchart to record some of their observations and to frame additional questions for investigation – for example:
◆ *Annie noticed that the roller-skate was stopped by the carpet strip.*
◆ *We all agreed that the blue car slowed down before the ball.*
◆ *Why does the car slow down more quickly on the carpet?* (The children might answer: 'Because the texture of the carpet is rough', 'Because the carpet rubs against the car', 'Because the car's wheels are too small to travel easily across the carpet', and so on.)

Now look at the bicycle with brakes. Talk to the children about how we can slow ourselves down when riding bikes and other ride-on toys. Discuss the use of brakes and any other methods the children suggest. What other forms of transport can the children think of that have brakes? Record their ideas

on the flipchart for future use.

Over several sessions, allow the children to use the 'ride-on' toys and to play with the collection of freewheeling toys. Maintain the focus of your questioning on the way that things slow down. Take photographs of the children playing.

When all the children have investigated how different toys slow down, draw them all together to look at the photographs. Agree on a suitable caption for each photograph, drawn from the flipchart notes (for example: 'The bicycle slows down when the brake pad rubs against the wheel').

Now look at the 'Birthday party' poster:
◆ *Which children in the picture might want to speed up or slow down?*
◆ *What would they say? (For example, 'I want to go faster'.)*
◆ *Could you add speech bubbles to the poster? (Use Post-it Notes.)*

ASSESSMENT

Ask individual children to show you how they can slow themselves down on the ride-on toys. Can they explain how their method of slowing down works? For those who are able to explain, extend the questioning to the freewheeling toys: *Why do some toys slow down more quickly than others?*

IDEAS FOR DISPLAY

Display the photographs of the children at play, with appropriate captions (see above).

IDEAS FOR DIFFERENTIATION

To support children who may not have developed the concept of slowing down, allow time for supervised play with the toys. More able children could be

challenged to ride the toys on a variety of different surfaces; do they notice how the different surfaces influence the way in which the toys slow down?

EXTENSION WORK

◆ Ask the children to suggest ways in which a toy (such as a roller skate) could be slowed down. Can they think of a way in which the toy could be made to slow down and then stop at exactly the same place every time?
◆ Provide a range of different surfaces for the children to investigate. Which surface makes the toys slow down the most?

INVESTIGATING HOW BALLOONS MOVE

GROUP SIZE AND ORGANIZATION
Whole class.
DURATION
Up to one hour.
LEARNING OBJECTIVE
To know that forces can make things change shape, speed up, slow down or change direction.

YOU WILL NEED

The 'Birthday party' poster; enough 'spherical' balloons to allow one per child or pair (most of them should be inflated ready for use); a balloon pump; rolled-up newspapers or magazines; access to a large space (the hall, playground or sports field); copies of photocopiable page 21.

SAFETY

Children can choke on balloons if they are allowed to blow them up by mouth. We strongly recommend the use of a balloon pump and the provision of additional adult support for this lesson.

WHAT TO DO

Look at the 'Birthday party' poster together. Focus the children's attention on the balloons. Find out what they know about balloons:
◆ *What games do you like to play with balloons?*
◆ *How would the balloons move if they were tied up outside in the breeze?*
◆ *What gives the balloon its shape?*
Talk to the children about a deflated balloon. Use the

FORCES AND MOTION

language of forces (*push, pull, change shape*) to help them describe what happens when a balloon is inflated. *What is being forced into the balloon when the pump is squeezed?*

Let different children take turns at blowing up a balloon. Help them to explain where the forces are acting. *Where can you feel the force as you pump?* (Pushing against their hands/making their muscles work.) *Where can you see the force changing the shape of the balloon?* (The balloon is getting bigger/is stretching/is rounder/is longer/the skin is tighter and so on.)

Add the balloons that the children have blown up to the collection of balloons that you have already inflated. Take them to the hall (or if the weather is very calm, go outside) where the children can play with them safely. After a little free play, draw the class together and set some individual challenges:

◆ *Can anyone make a balloon travel in a straight line?*
◆ *Can anyone keep the balloon in the air while I count to 5...10... 20?*
◆ *How many different ways can you find to make your balloon change direction?*
◆ *How can you make your balloon speed up and slow down?*

The children can use rolled-up magazines as bats to extend their control over the balloons.

To draw the lesson together, show the children a copy of photocopiable page 21 and explain that they have to draw the path taken by their balloon. If necessary, draw an example on the board (perhaps based on the top panel of page 21).

ASSESSMENT

Talk to the children about the ways they have used forces to make the balloons speed up, slow down and change direction. Which children can describe the relationship between their own actions and the resulting change in movement of the balloon? Who can relate the amount of force used to the resulting change in movement of the balloon?

IDEAS FOR DISPLAY

Cut out coloured paper in the shape of balloons. Display the direction words 'up' and 'down' and the movement words 'speed up' and 'slow down' near the balloon shapes. The children can use chalk to draw in the flight paths of the balloons to show how they made them change direction.

IDEAS FOR DIFFERENTIATION

For children requiring support, this activity can be repeated using a wide variety of objects. You could try airflow balls, table tennis balls and bean bags. Each time, the children should be encouraged to describe the flight of the object in terms of speeding up, slowing down and changing direction.

More able children can add direction and movement words to their photocopiable sheet, and help to plan the display. Ask them to think about the different ways in which they could make the balloon change direction, such as fanning it along the floor using a magazine or keeping it in the air using different body parts.

EXTENSION WORK

In subsequent lessons, you could provide balloons of different shapes and sizes. Ask the children to predict how the size or shape will make a difference to the flight of the balloons. Will the balloons change direction in the same way as the balloons the children have already used?

RESOURCE BANK

FORCES AND MOTION

SWINGBALL

GROUP SIZE AND ORGANIZATION
Whole class in groups of 8–10, following three activities in rotation.
DURATION
40–60 minutes.
LEARNING OBJECTIVE
To understand that when things speed up, slow down or change direction, there is a cause.

YOU WILL NEED
The 'Birthday party' poster; access to an area of grass on a day with fine weather; a swingball and racquets; five inflated balloons; ten 1m lengths of string or lightweight cord; photocopiable page 22; some different-sized airflow balls.

SAFETY
Ensure that the swingball set is securely driven into the soil (unless it has a weighted base). The swingball activity will require additional adult supervision. Make sure that the children have sufficient space to carry out the practical activities without bumping into each other.

WHAT TO DO
Look at the 'Birthday party' poster together. Focus the children's attention on the swingball game. Find out what the children know about this game:
◆ *What makes the ball travel around the pole?*
◆ *How can you make the ball change direction?*
Now take a balloon and tie it to your wrist with a length of string. Grip the string in your hand and swing the balloon through the air. Show the children that you can make the balloon change direction without touching it.
◆ *What is making the balloon change direction?*
◆ *What makes it go faster? What makes it go slower?*
Allow a small number of children to try this. Can they make the balloon speed up, slow down and change direction? Ask them to describe what they are doing, using the words 'pull' and 'swing'.
Now take the class outside to look at the swingball set. Ask first one child and then a pair of children to demonstrate it. Ask the class to focus on the way the ball is moving. Leave a group of 8–10 children outside to work with the swingball. An additional adult should ensure that pairs of children take turns at the game while the others watch and describe the movement of the ball. He or she should ask questions:

◆ *What is pushing the ball?*
◆ *Does it always travel in the same direction?*
◆ *What makes the ball change direction?*
Divide the rest of the children into two groups. Send one group to their seats, where they can complete photocopiable page 22 by adding an arrow to the swingball picture and writing a sentence to describe what makes the ball change direction. The remaining children can work with you in the classroom to investigate the movement of balloons on strings. Can they invent a game using the balloons? Encourage them to think about their own and others' safety. Ask them what they think would happen if the balloons were replaced by airflow balls.
Rotate the groups at 10-minute intervals.
Finally, draw all the children together to discuss their experiences. Ask some children to explain how they completed the photocopiable sheet. Choose some other children to demonstrate their invented game.

ASSESSMENT
As the lesson progresses, note those children who are able to use vocabulary such as 'push', 'pull', 'speed up', 'slow down' and 'change direction' in the correct contexts. Compare their oral responses with their recorded work on the photocopiable sheet.

IDEAS FOR DISPLAY
Paint a picture of a swingball, cut it out and stick it in the middle of a display board. Add arrows to the

board showing the direction of movement of the ball. Add appropriate vocabulary and examples of the children's completed photocopiable sheets.

IDEAS FOR DIFFERENTIATION
Differentiation will be largely by outcome. If possible, provide support by creating smaller groups for those children who may need help with the language content of the lesson. More able children could be challenged with the extension activity below.

EXTENSION WORK
Airflow balls come in a variety of sizes. Use different-sized balls to extend the children's prediction skills: *What would happen if we changed this airflow ball for a larger/smaller one – will there be a difference? Why?*

PUSHES AND SQUASHES

GROUP SIZE AND ORGANIZATION
Whole class, then groups.
DURATION
45 minutes.
LEARNING OBJECTIVE
To know that forces can change the shape of an object.

YOU WILL NEED
The 'Birthday party' poster; balloons, including a few inflated ones; a balloon pump; Unifix or other plastic cubes; photocopiable page 23; scissors; sorting hoops; a wine cork; a bouncy castle (optional). Prepare a varied collection of balls; include some balls that cannot be squashed at all (such as cricket balls) and some balls of Plasticine or modelling dough.

SAFETY
Care needs to be taken with the cork-firing activity, which is included as a teacher demonstration.

WHAT TO DO
Look at the 'Birthday party' poster. Draw the children's attention to the bouncy castle. Talk about what it feels like to go on a bouncy castle. Can the children describe the way the castle pushes them up in the air? Ask a few children to demonstrate what happens as they bounce on the castle. Relate their movements to the bouncy castle in the picture.

Now blow up a balloon. Ask the children to consider how the balloon is like a bouncy castle. Do the children know that the castle is full of air? Show them that you are filling the balloon with air, and draw the parallel with the bouncy castle.

Ask the children to think about the ways in which bouncing on the bouncy castle makes it change shape. Show them that the balloon can be squashed and that

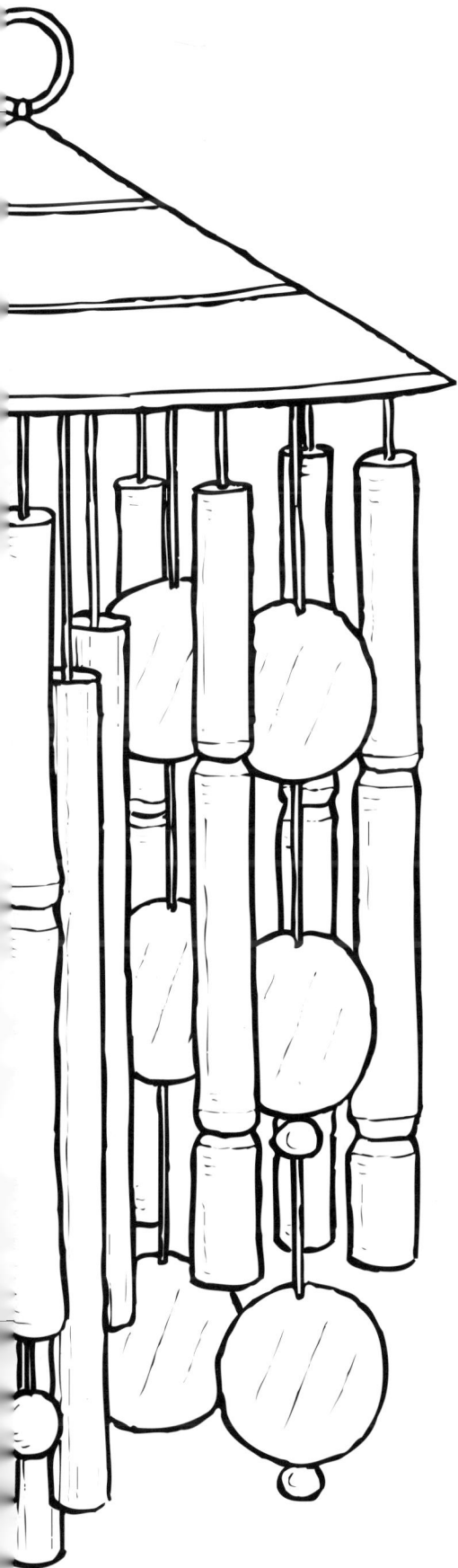

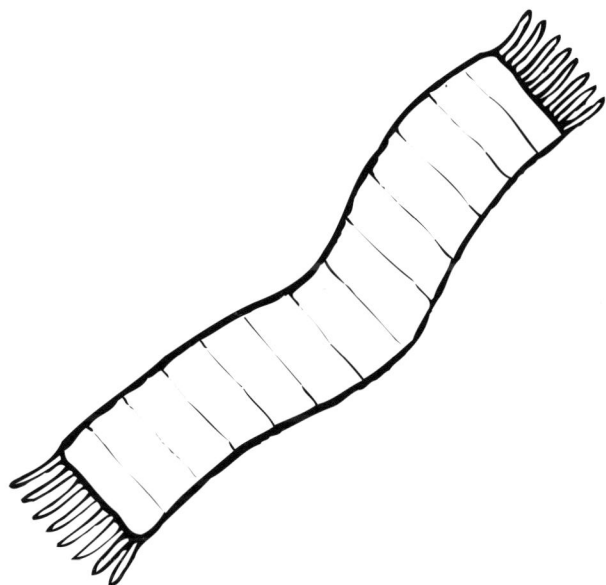

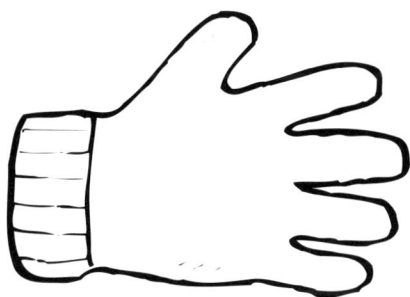

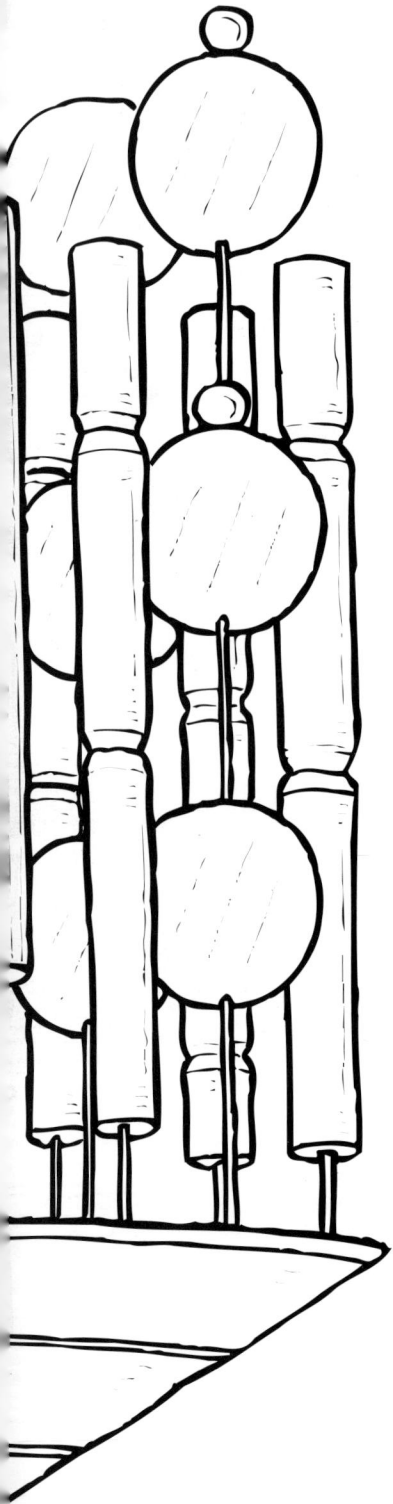

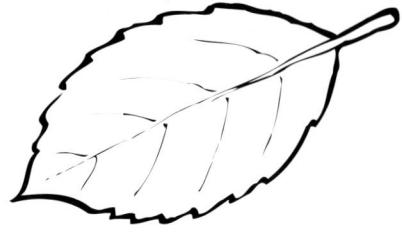

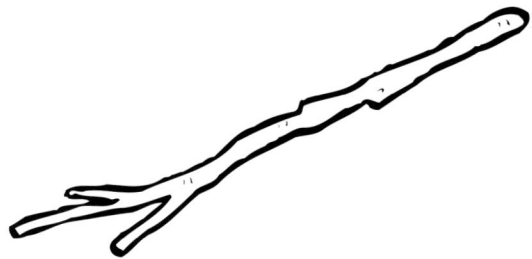

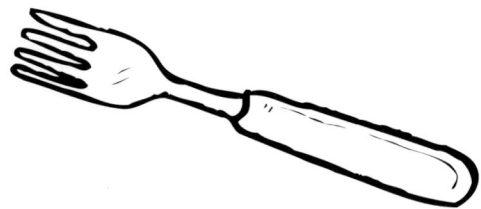

it returns to its original shape. Give a few children the chance to repeat this. Ask them to explain the pushes: they are pushing down on the balloon, and the balloon is pushing back up at them.

All the class can pretend that they have a balloon and play a 'follow-my-leader' game to show what would happen if they squashed their balloons (including bursting them).

Now split the class into two groups. Group 1 can complete the sequencing sheet (photocopiable page 23). Group 2 can sort the collection of balls into hoops. Ask them to justify their sorting. Encourage them to use the sorting criteria 'can be squashed'/ 'cannot be squashed'. Help them to record their sorting.

When both groups have completed both of the activities, draw the lesson to a close by demonstrating the pushing power of the balloons. Push a wine-bottle cork down into the (sealed) neck of an inflated balloon, then release the neck suddenly: the balloon will 'fire' the cork out.

ASSESSMENT
Identify those children who are able to explain the movement of people on a bouncy castle and the movement of the cork in terms of 'pushes'.

IDEAS FOR DISPLAY
The sorted collection of balls can form an interactive display. Try changing the criterion for the sorting, and ask the children to guess or choose from a range of possible criteria (colour, bounciness, size, shape, weight, material and so on).

IDEAS FOR DIFFERENTIATION
At the point in the lesson where the children are split into groups, it is possible to create ability groups so that more able children are extended and less able children supported in the activities. If you have an additional adult in the classroom, you may wish to create a smaller sub-group for the sorting activity. The photocopiable sheet can be modified for younger or less able children by removing the bottom two squares.

EXTENSION WORK
More able children may understand that the firing or pushing power of the balloon relates to the fact that the balloon tends to return to its original (round) shape. Can they list other items they know of that can be squashed and will then return to their original shapes? (For example: balls, tyres, bouncy castles, foam cushions, cuddly toys.)

A VISIT TO THE PARK

GROUP SIZE AND ORGANIZATION
Whole-class visit; activities in groups of up to four.
DURATION
About 40 minutes (more if free play is allowed), plus travelling time.
LEARNING OBJECTIVE
To reinforce the concepts and language of forces developed in previous lessons by using them in a new context.

YOU WILL NEED
One ball (such as a tennis ball) for each small group; access to a park that contains a range of moving and static play equipment (such as a see-saw, roundabout, slide, climbing frame and swings).

You will need additional adult support to address the issues raised in your risk assessment. In our school, we would expect one adult to supervise each small group; for a class of 30, we would require a minimum of eight adults (including the teacher). The additional adults should be prepared for the trip by being given clear safety instructions and advice on the specific language and concepts that you are trying to reinforce in this lesson (see 'What to do').

SAFETY
We strongly recommend that you follow your school or LEA guidelines concerning park visits. We suggest that you carry out your own risk assessment and share your findings with all those taking part in the visit. As

part of the risk assessment, you should consider what additional safety rules (beyond those that normally apply in the classroom or playground) should be given to the children.

As with any visit, you may need to consider: exposure to sunlight; drinks; toilets; inhalers and other medication; first aid. The balls should be carried in a suitable bag to prevent them being dropped on the journey.

WHAT TO DO

Before leaving the school, gather the children and adult helpers together. Tell the children that they are going to the park, and that as they try out the different pieces of play equipment they will be learning about forces.

Say that they will be using the language of forces to describe what they see and do in the park. What words can they think of that describe the movement

of things? Help them by reminding them of words used in previous lessons: up, down, forwards, backwards, fast, slow, speed up, slow down, stop, start.

They will also be describing the way that different pushes and pulls act on them. It is important that your adult helpers know they will be asking the children questions such as:

◆ Can you feel any pushes or pulls?
◆ Where can you feel the force?
◆ How does the force change when you speed up/slow down?

Reinforce any safety issues that you feel would be best dealt with at this time, then set off to the park.

On arrival at the park, reinforce your safety rules with the children. Now apply the language developed at school to the moving equipment:

◆ The swings swing.
◆ The roundabout turns.
◆ How does the see-saw move?

Tell your children that the adult helpers will watch them as they try out different pieces of play equipment, and that they will be asked to describe the forces they can feel in each type of movement that they make.

Split the children into their groups and send them to different pieces of play equipment. If there are insufficient pieces of play equipment for all the groups, create extra activities using the balls.

After a few minutes, call all the groups together near a see-saw or roundabout. Talk to them about the forces they have felt. Ask them to describe what happens when they speed up or slow down.

Now rotate the groups, giving each group a few minutes on each piece of equipment. This should give you the opportunity to circulate and ask the children questions that will reveal their understanding.

ASSESSMENT

Note those children who are able/unable to use the language of forces correctly in the context of the park activities.

IDEAS FOR DIFFERENTIATION

Help children who have poorly developed language skills by phrasing questions in simple terms: Can you feel a push? Where can you feel it?

EXTENSION WORK

Use a ball on the roundabout or see-saw to demonstrate the forces acting there. Ask:

◆ What happens to the ball?
◆ What happens to the ball if the roundabout/see-saw is moved more quickly?

FORCES AND MOTION

Name _____ Date _____

How things move

◆ Choose a word to complete these sentences:

The _____ bounced on the playground.

The _____ flew through the air.

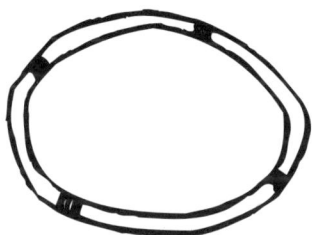   

hoop   ball   beanbag   skittle

◆ Describe the way the hoops moved.

_____

_____

_____

◆ Draw the skittles being hit by the ball.

Name —————————————   Date —————————————

Table football

When I played table football, I ————————————————

——————————————————————————————

——————————————————————————————

——————————————————————————————

——————————————————————————————

The air ———————————————————————

PHOTOCOPIABLE
RESOURCE
BANK

FORCES AND MOTION

Name _____   Date _____

Balloons

Serena's balloon made this pathway:

◆ Draw your balloon's pathway:

◆ Use these words to describe how your balloon travelled:

speed up   slow down   go up   go down

bounce   push

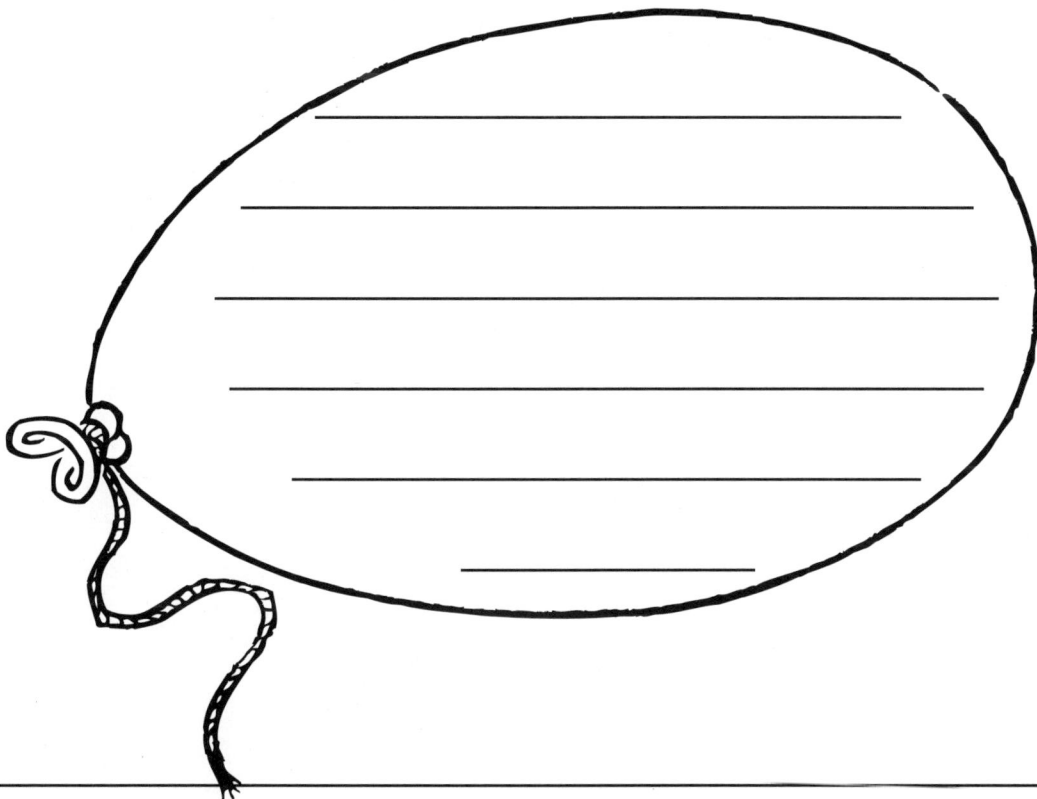

PHOTOCOPIABLE
RESOURCE
BANK

FORCES AND MOTION

Name _____ Date _____

Swingball

◆ Draw an arrow to show the ball's pathway.

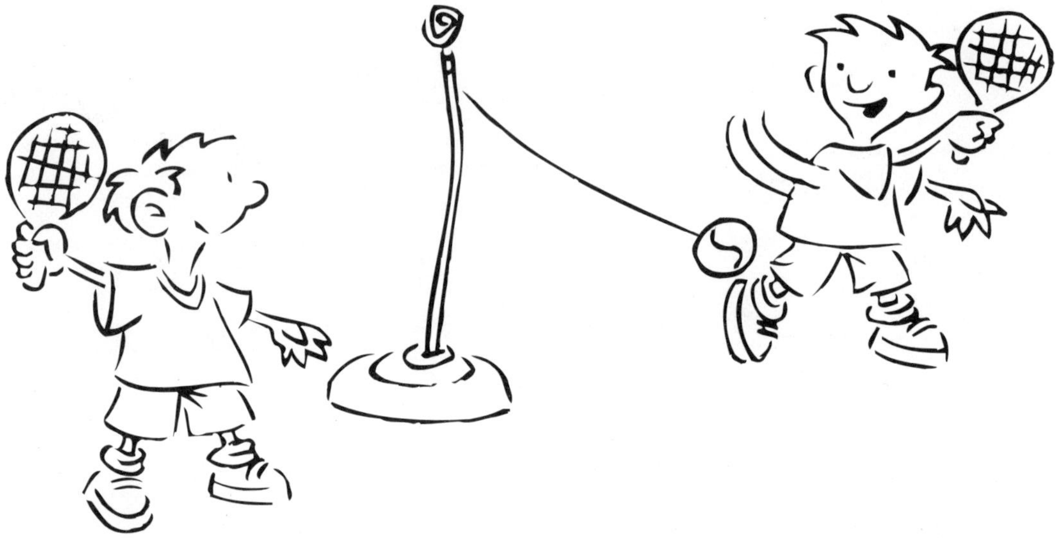

◆ Explain what makes the ball change direction.

The ball changes direction when _____

_____

_____

_____

_____

_____

Name —————————— Date ——————————

Bouncy castle

◆ Cut out the pictures and stick them in order.

PHOTOCOPIABLE
RESOURCE
BANK

LIGHT AND SOUND

THE LIGHT WALK

GROUP SIZE AND ORGANIZATION
Whole class (smaller groups if additional support is available).
DURATION
40 minutes.
LEARNING OBJECTIVE
To know that lights can have different colours and are used for different purposes.

YOU WILL NEED
The 'Birthday party' poster (both sides); A3-sized photocopies (one per child) of the 'Fairground' mini-poster; brightly coloured pens or crayons.

WHAT TO DO
Look at the 'Birthday party' poster together. Encourage the children to identify lights in the picture. Discuss the colours that you can see (with Reception children, you might like to extend this part of the lesson to work on colour recognition). Talk to the children about what the lights are being used for; encourage the idea that the candles are lights, as well as the electric bulbs. Now look at the 'Living room' and 'Kitchen' mini-posters to see examples of LED lights. Discuss what colour these would be in real life (red or green). The children can then have a look around the classroom to find lights and identify their use.

As a class (or in smaller groups if you have appropriate support), walk around your school looking for similar lights. The school office and any ICT areas are good places to look.

On returning to the classroom, look at the 'Fairground' mini-poster; talk about how fairground lights are used to make a colourful and attractive display (particularly in the dark), encouraging you to go on their ride. Give the children their own copy of the fairground picture and ask them to colour the lights they can see in with bright colours.

ASSESSMENT
There are opportunities for teacher assessment during the initial discussion and throughout the walk around the school. The children's fairground pictures will give you a good indication of their ability to recognize a light source.

IDEAS FOR DISPLAY
The completed fairground pictures can be displayed.

IDEAS FOR DIFFERENTIATION
The children will be naturally differentiated by their observational skills. It is important to make sure that all the children are involved in the observation activity.

EXTENSION WORK
The children could go on to observe other lights: at home, in a car, in the street and so on. Give appropriate warnings about not standing in the road – most of the lights they will see there indicate danger!

SEEING COLOURS IN THE DARK

GROUP SIZE AND ORGANIZATION
Whole class, then groups of five or six.
DURATION
40 minutes.
LEARNING OBJECTIVE
To know that some materials are easier to see in the dark than others.

YOU WILL NEED
Pieces of coloured material with a good variety of light and dark colours, including some fluorescent colours; shoeboxes (one per group, preferably all the same kind) with a hole cut in one end and lift-off lids, so that they look quite dark (but not pitch black) inside when the lid is on – it may be necessary to cut an additional hole in the lid to allow a small amount of light in.

LIGHT AND SOUND

WHAT TO DO

Explain to the children that you would like them to find out which is the safest colour sweater to wear for walking home in the early evening in winter. Establish that this means the most visible in dim light.

Discuss the colours of the pieces of material (with a Reception class, you may like to spend quite a long time identifying the colours). Ask the children to predict which would be the most visible. To make sure that the children are thinking independently, it might be better to take a written ballot.

Now discuss how they could test their prediction using the box. Talk about how the test can be made fair. They need to understand that only one thing should be changed in the test: the piece of material. Allow the children, working in small groups, to test the materials by looking in to the shoebox at each piece of material in turn. Explain that the result of the test relies on a subjective judgement, but that they can make it more reliable by repeating the test with a different child looking through the shoebox.

If you wish, the children can do some simple recording following this investigation. The following headings should be addressed when encouraging children to record:
◆ We are finding out... [investigating]
◆ We need... [equipment]
◆ We think... [predicting]
◆ We discovered... [results]
Emphasis on style is important: the writing should state clearly and accurately what has happened.

ASSESSMENT

There are opportunities for teacher assessment throughout this lesson. The key assessment areas should be the children's understanding of a fair test and their ability to predict results independently. Any written work can also be used for assessment.

IDEAS FOR DISPLAY

The resources for this activity could be used in an interactive table display, perhaps with a wider variety of materials (including reflective materials) and a torch to shine in to the shoebox.

IDEAS FOR DIFFERENTIATION

More able children could test materials which are relatively similar in colour; less able children could test markedly different-coloured pieces of material.

EXTENSION WORK

The children could go on to test whether it is better to have strips of bright material on clothing or for the clothing to be made completely out of the bright material, using a torch shone in to the shoebox; reflective materials could be included in this test.

HALL OF MIRRORS

GROUP SIZE AND ORGANIZATION
Whole class.
DURATION
40 minutes.
LEARNING OBJECTIVE
To know that light travels in straight lines and can be reflected.

YOU WILL NEED

The 'Living room' mini-poster; plastic mirrors; targets (home-made or bought) with a bullseye and an outer ring. Find a room that can be darkened (a hall is ideal); install the targets and several bright, direct light sources (lamps or torches) so that the children will be able to direct the lights onto the targets with mirrors; and draw wiggly pathways on display paper on the walls (or with chalk on the floor).

SAFETY

It is important to use plastic mirrors, not glass ones.

WHAT TO DO

Look at the 'Living room' mini-poster and find the mirror. Discuss the children's experience of mirrors, and make sure that they do not perceive the mirror as a light source. Ask:

LIGHT AND SOUND

◆ *What are mirrors used for?*
◆ *Where do we usually find mirrors?*

In the hall, give the children the mirrors (ideally one each) and ask them to say what they can see in it. They will need encouragement to see the wider picture rather than just their own reflection. Encourage them to walk around and observe their friends in the mirrors. You can then darken the room and turn on the light sources. The children can use their mirrors to flash the light around the room.

Bring the children together at this point and draw their attention to the targets that have been strategically placed around the room. They can practise using their mirrors to reflect the light onto the targets, trying to get a bullseye. They are not allowed to move the light sources. This activity could be done in groups of two or three, with the children racing each other to hit the targets. This will be fast and furious, but enormous fun!

The children can try to explain what is happening with the light and how they are able to reflect it. You can discuss reflective materials, and identify which materials reflect best.

Ask the children to use their mirrors to trace the wiggly lines on the walls or the floor. *Is this easier or more difficult the nearer the light source you are, or does it make no difference? How about if you stand to the side?* You can make this much harder by having a flashing light source.

Talk to the children about where the light is coming from (the light sources, not the mirrors). See whether they can explain what is happening to the light (reflection) and whether they have seen this happen at any other time (for example, bright sunlight on a window).

ASSESSMENT

Move around the hall, asking the children how the light is getting from the light source to the floor or wall. Note whether they say that it is reflected.

IDEAS FOR DISPLAY

Create an interactive display in the classroom. This could include mirrors (and other reflective surfaces), torches and targets. Displaying various pathways on the walls can encourage diverse play experiences.

IDEAS FOR DIFFERENTIATION

Less able children should require little support with this activity; however, their language and conceptual development will be enhanced if additional adult support is available to discuss the activity with them.

More able children can be asked to pair up and use two mirrors to see the backs of their own heads. They will need to work together to achieve this. When they have succeeded, they can be encouraged to make a 'human periscope' that will enable them to see around corners or over walls!

LIGHT AND SOUND

MAKING SHADOWS

GROUP SIZE AND ORGANIZATION
Whole class.
DURATION
Two 30-minute sessions on the same day.
LEARNING OBJECTIVE
To know that shadows change through the day.

YOU WILL NEED
The 'Birthday party' poster; playground chalk; rulers or tape measures; additional adult support; a sunny day.

SAFETY
The children need to be taught **never** to look directly at the Sun. The dangers of sunburn could be also discussed.

WHAT TO DO
Start with a morning session. Look at the 'Birthday party' poster and point out the shadows by the bouncy castle. *Are there any others?* Explain that you can tell the time of day from a shadow, because shadows move as the Sun crosses the sky. Go out into the playground; ask the children, in pairs, to draw around each other's shadows with playground chalk. They should each mark their own position with an 'X' and their initials. Encourage the children to be aware of the Sun's position in the sky, making sure they don't look directly at it.

Later in the day, go out again; ask the children to stand once more on their own X mark. Can they get their present shadow to match the position of the one they drew earlier? In the same pairs, they can redraw the shadows using chalk as before. Ask them to describe in their own words how the shadows have changed, perhaps measuring and comparing the lengths. *Where has the sun moved to?*

Ask the children to predict what their shadow would be like first thing in the morning, at midday and at the end of the evening. Encourage them to explain their predictions.

Look again at the 'Birthday party' poster, and see whether the children can guess roughly what time of day it is by looking at the shadows on the picture. Ask: *What will happen to the shadows later in the day?*

ASSESSMENT
This activity will stimulate a lot of spontaneous discussion among the children. From this, you should be able to assess whether they understand the idea of the Sun moving through the day. *Where did the Sun start from? Where did it move to?*

IDEAS FOR DISPLAY
Draw a graph or chart of the recorded shadow lengths, using an ICT program such as *Graphplot*.

IDEAS FOR DIFFERENTIATION
With Year 2 children, you could measure the shadows and see how much longer or shorter they become; the children could try to predict how long their shadows might be first thing in the morning and last thing at night. Year 1 children could use non-standard measures; Reception children may need help to draw around the shadows accurately.

EXTENSION WORK
◆ Using an OHP, the children can make shadow puppets with their hands, or with cardboard cut-outs stuck onto pieces of thin dowel. They could make a simple shadow puppet theatre from a cardboard box with tissue paper across the front, and use it to show the Sun moving across the sky or the Earth and other planets going around the Sun.
◆ Traditional stories concerning the movement of the Sun (such as 'How the beaver got his tail') are often fascinating for children following this activity.

LIGHT AND SOUND

A SOUND MOBILE

GROUP SIZE AND ORGANIZATION
Whole class, then pairs or small groups.
DURATION
60 minutes.
LEARNING OBJECTIVE
To experience the different sounds made by different materials.

YOU WILL NEED
The 'Wind chimes' mini-poster; a commercial wind chime; some strong twigs. Collect various objects that can produce clanging sounds, such as keys, pieces of copper piping, old cutlery and key-rings, along with the odd inappropriate item such as a glove or wooden spoon. (We have always found that a letter to parents produces amazing things for this activity.)

SAFETY
The children should be reminded not to put the resources into their mouths.

WHAT TO DO
Show the children your commercial wind chime. Listen to the sounds it makes, and how these sounds vary according to how much force is used to make it move. (If you hang the wind chime on a string, it is easy to swing it back and forth.) Look at the materials used to make it. Use the 'Wind chimes' mini-poster to discuss what materials would or would not be effective for making a wind chime.

Show the children the collection of items. Ask small groups or pairs to select some items and make their own wind chime. The younger the children are, the more you may need to prepare ahead of the lesson in order to allow them to work independently. For example, we have found that Reception children needed to have strings attached to the items so that they only had to tie them on to a prepared mobile (two twigs, already joined and balanced for them). Year 1 children could attach items, but also needed to have the twigs joined; Year 2 children could join up the two twigs, but needed help to put the strings on to hang up the mobile.

ASSESSMENT
Can the children explain to you what makes the chime louder or quieter, and describe the sounds it makes? Can they select appropriate materials to make a wind chime?

IDEAS FOR DISPLAY
The children's wind chimes look great hung from the ceiling; in the summer, with the windows open, they make a wonderful sound. We have also used the chimes as part of an art exhibition.

IDEAS FOR DIFFERENTIATION
To make the lesson more challenging, ask the children to construct a square with twigs instead of a cross. This type of mobile is harder to balance, and the hanging of chimes needs to be more precise to make a good sound.

EXTENSION WORK
The children could go on to compare the sounds of their chimes with the sounds of commercial ones. They could work out the difference in cost between the home-made chimes and shop-bought chimes.

THE LOUDEST RAINMAKER

GROUP SIZE AND ORGANIZATION
Whole class, then groups of five or six.
DURATION
Two 40-minute sessions.
LEARNING OBJECTIVES
To make a loud instrument. To use a fair test.

YOU WILL NEED
The 'Kitchen' and 'Living room' mini-posters; a collection of recycled materials, including tubes, paper and boxes; sticky tape; adhesive; elastic bands; a variety of materials for shaking (seeds, beans, pasta, and so on).

LIGHT AND SOUND

SAFETY
Remind the children not to put dry beans, lentils and so on into their mouths, noses or ears. It is also important not to use red kidney beans, as these are poisonous before they are soaked.

WHAT TO DO
Session 1
With the children together on the carpet, look at the 'Kitchen' and 'Living room' mini-posters. Discuss the things that make a noise and the reasons why they do so – for example, the microwave goes 'ping' to tell you it has stopped heating the food.

Explain that we and other cultures make noises for many different reasons. Many cultures in the past used rain dances to encourage the rains to come. In these dances, 'rainmakers' were used: instruments with a loud shaker-type sound.

Ask the children to have a go at making the loudest rainmaker they can – the opportunity to make noise is always very popular! However, remind them that voices cannot be part of a rainmaker. Allow groups to make their own instrument from the materials available; explain that the rainmakers will be tested to find the loudest.

Session 2
When testing the rainmakers, it is important to make the test as fair as possible. Discuss with the children how this can be achieved; encourage them to identify difficulties that could make the test unfair. We all have slightly different levels of hearing, and could shake or tip the rainmakers at different speeds or with different amounts of force. Some ideas to help make this a fair test are:

◆ An adult tests all of the rainmakers, so that the speed of tipping is approximately the same.
◆ No names are included on them, so the children do not just support their friends.
◆ Put the instruments in groups and have a winner from each group going forward to a final.
◆ Do the test outside, moving away from the children until they can't hear the instrument any more; then compare the distances. As a further safeguard, do not let the children see which instrument you are using.
◆ A combination of the above!
When you have determined which is the loudest rainmaker, discuss with the children what features of the instrument make it effective (for example: space for the beans to move; a plastic rather than wooden or card container).

ASSESSMENT
During discussion, assess (and record) which children understand the process of a fair test.

IDEAS FOR DISPLAY
The rainmakers will make a superbly noisy interactive display in the classroom – if you can stand it!

IDEAS FOR DIFFERENTIATION
Challenge more able children to sort appropriate from inappropriate materials, and let them carry out the test independently.

EXTENSION WORK
The children could test various natural materials (such as stones and bark chippings) to see whether any make a louder rainmaker than the materials they have already tried.

LIGHT AND SOUND

ANIMAL EARS

GROUP SIZE AND ORGANIZATION
Whole class.
DURATION
40 minutes.
LEARNING OBJECTIVES
To know that sound is heard when it goes into the ear. To know that some animals have ears that are specially adapted to hear more acutely.

YOU WILL NEED
The 'Birthday party' poster; the 'Living room' mini-poster; a wooden block and beater; a selection of pictures of animals, including an elephant, a rabbit, a human, a frog, and two dogs – one with long ears (such as a bassett-hound or cocker spaniel) and one with short ears (such as a Jack Russell); photocopiable pages 31 and 32; a musical instrument.

SAFETY
This activity provides a good opportunity to remind the children how fragile the ear is, and that you should never poke anything into it or shout close to someone's ear.

WHAT TO DO
Look at the 'Birthday party' poster together; encourage the children to identify things in the picture that make a sound (the skittles and ball, the electric drill, the bouncing child and so on). You might like to consider the various sound-making things in the 'Living room' mini-poster as well. Use discussion to get an idea of what the children already know about sound and hearing. Explain that sound is heard when it enters the ear. For Year 2 children, you may like to explain that sound is transmitted through the bones inside the ear.

Ask the children to listen to you striking the wooden block with the beater; then ask them to listen again with their hands firmly over their ears. Ask: *What is the difference?* Explain that it is much harder for the sound to get into the ear when the hand is covering it.

Now show them the animal pictures. Discuss why elephants have big ears (to keep them cool by flapping), and why rabbits move their ears (so they can pinpoint exactly where a sound is coming from). *Do frogs have ears?* (Yes, but no ear flaps – there is a sound opening just under and behind each eye.) Show the two dog pictures together, explaining that some differences are simply created by breeding for visual appeal – dogs with small ears can hear just as well as dogs with big ears).

Now talk about human ears. Can the children wiggle their ears? Explain that some people can do this, but it is quite rare. Each individual within an animal species has slightly different characteristics. The children can look at each other's ears and observe similarities and differences.

Give out copies of one or both of photocopiable pages 31 and 32, as appropriate (see 'Ideas for differentiation'). Ask the children to complete the matching task.

ASSESSMENT
There are opportunities for teacher assessment in the initial discussion, and in discussion throughout the lesson – for example, later on, you could ask: *What are ears used for?* The photocopiable sheets are designed to be fun, and do not provide assessment information.

IDEAS FOR DISPLAY
Display the collection of ear pictures with separate labels (such as 'Elephant ear'), so that the children can play 'Misfits' with the display.

IDEAS FOR DIFFERENTIATION
Use both photocopiable sheets, distributed appropriately. Younger or less able children could match ear pictures to animals; older or more able children could match sentences to animals.

EXTENSION WORK
◆ The children can carry out further work on the ear – for example, learning about its structure (the outer ear is made of cartilage, the middle ear has bones to transmit sounds, the inner ear has sensitive hairs to pick up vibrations.
◆ They can investigate how sounds become fainter when they are further away. This could be linked to the 'loudest rainmaker' test (see page 28).

RESOURCE BANK

Name _____   Date _____

Animal ears: pictures

◆ Match each ear to the correct animal.

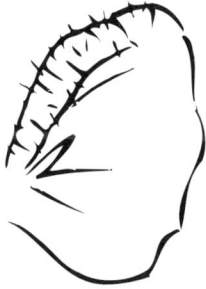

PHOTOCOPIABLE
RESOURCE
BANK

Name ————————————————   Date ————————————————

Animal ears: sentences

◆ Match each sentence to the correct animal.

| They can move their ears backwards and forwards. |

| They have a small ear hole near each eye. |

| They flap their ears to keep cool. |

| Some can wiggle their ears. |

| They can move their ears to pinpoint sounds. |

| Their ears may be all kinds of different shapes. |

PHOTOCOPIABLE
RESOURCE
BANK